The Godmother of Crime

The True Story of Joan Hannington
– From Jewel Thief to Icon

Lucy Loophole

Copyright © 2024 by Lucy Loophole

All rights reserved. No part of this publication may be reproduced, distributed, or transmitted in any form or by any means, including photocopying, recording, or other electronic or mechanical methods, without the prior written permission of the publisher, except in the case of brief quotations embodied in critical reviews and certain other noncommercial uses permitted by copyright law.

Table of Contents

Introduction

Chapter 1: From Trauma to Triumph

Chapter 2: London in the 1980s – A Crime-Fueled City

Chapter 3: The Heist Queen Emerges

Chapter 4: The Glamour and Grit of Crime

Chapter 5: Power, Fame, and the Cost of Crime

Chapter 6: Life Beyond the Heists

Chapter 7: From Infamy to Pop Culture Icon

Chapter 8: The Godmother's Legacy

Chapter 9: Joan Today

Chapter 10: The Enduring Fascination with Female Criminals

Conclusion: The Price of Power

Introduction

In the shadowy, adrenaline-fueled streets of 1980s London, Joan Hannington carved out a name for herself as a figure both feared and admired. Known as "The Godmother" in criminal circles, Joan's life story is far from ordinary. Born into a world of hardship, she rose from an abusive childhood and a violent marriage to become one of the most notorious jewel thieves of her time. Her journey from victim to criminal mastermind, a tale filled with high-stakes heists, luxury, and danger, continues to captivate and intrigue audiences today.

The Godmother of Crime isn't just a story of crime; it is the story of **survival** and **power**. At its core is a woman who refused to be defined by her circumstances. In the male-dominated underworld of London, Joan's cunning and charm allowed her to outmaneuver those who underestimated her. Using unconventional methods, such as swallowing diamonds to evade capture, Joan's life became a high-wire act of calculated risks and bold decisions. Her rise through the criminal ranks was nothing short of audacious, and her ability to balance the dual roles of **motherhood** and **criminality** makes her story both complex and compelling.

But Joan's life is not merely a tale of glamour and grit. It is also a **study in resilience**. In an era when women were often confined by social expectations, Joan broke free, taking control of her destiny in ways that defied the norms of her time. Yet, the price of power in the underworld was steep. Her choices came at a heavy personal cost, particularly in her relationship with her daughter, Debbie, whose well-being was at the heart of Joan's every move—even when those moves pushed them further apart.

From her early forays into jewel theft to her eventual rise as a **pop culture icon**—immortalized in her memoir and the critically acclaimed 2024 ITV series *Joan*—this book delves deep into the life of a woman who lived on the edge of society, forever balancing danger with the need for survival.

As you turn the pages of *The Godmother of Crime*, you'll not only be drawn into the thrilling heists and dangerous escapades, but you'll also gain insight into the **emotional complexities** that come with a life of crime. Joan's story is one of **empowerment**—but also of loss, isolation, and the weight of the choices she made in pursuit of freedom. In the end, Joan Hannington is more than just a jewel thief; she is a symbol of **survival, power, and transformation**, whose legacy continues to influence both true crime narratives and the portrayal of female criminals in media today.

This is her story.

Chapter 1: From Trauma to Triumph

Joan was born in 1953 into a deeply dysfunctional family, the youngest of six children. Raised in a working-class household, her childhood was marked by **neglect and abuse**. Joan's father, a violent man with a temper, often lashed out at his children, while her mother struggled to provide any emotional support. This environment deprived Joan of the love and security most children require to thrive.

At a young age, Joan experienced the instability of life on the margins. Her family moved frequently, often in search of better opportunities, but they found little relief. Joan, yearning for safety, turned inward, learning to rely on herself. The absence of stable role models left her vulnerable, and the emotional scars from this period of her life would shape her relationships and choices as she grew older.

By her teens, Joan had already begun to develop a tough exterior, masking her vulnerabilities with confidence and defiance. She longed for an escape from her circumstances, but lacking a support system or formal education, her options were limited. Like many women in similar situations during the post-war period, Joan saw **marriage** as a potential route to a better life. What she didn't anticipate was how this decision would plunge her into a new cycle of **abuse and control**.

Joan married young, hoping to escape the chaos of her upbringing. Unfortunately, she found herself trapped in a **violent marriage**. Her husband, Gary, was manipulative and physically abusive, a man who dominated her life through fear and coercion. Much like her father, Gary used violence as a means of control, and Joan, now a young mother, felt increasingly isolated.

The cycle of abuse was relentless, leaving Joan in a state of **constant fear** for herself and her daughter, Debbie. Desperate to break free, she sought ways to protect her child from the violence she had endured. This period of Joan's life was marked by emotional turmoil, but it was also where the first signs of her fierce resilience emerged.

It was in this crucible of hardship that Joan began to consider her options. Leaving Gary meant leaving behind financial security and putting herself and her child in potential danger, yet staying meant continuing to live in fear. With few resources available to her—no formal education and no means of financial independence—Joan began to take drastic steps. The pressures of her abusive marriage, coupled with her need to protect Debbie, would later fuel the **desperation** that led her to a life of crime.

Her relationship with Gary was not just a personal struggle but a reflection of the broader social dynamics of the time. In the 1970s, women like Joan had few legal protections against domestic violence, and the stigma surrounding divorce and single motherhood was profound. Joan's decisions during this period were shaped by her environment, pushing her to seek survival by any means necessary.

The birth of her daughter, Debbie, marked a turning point in Joan's life. Motherhood deepened her sense of responsibility, and her primary motivation became securing a better future for her child. But providing for Debbie in the face of poverty, domestic violence, and limited opportunities was a constant struggle. Joan's early experiences of neglect made her fiercely determined to be a better mother, and this drive shaped many of her decisions in the years to come.

It was this protective instinct that led Joan to make the radical choice to leave her abusive husband and seek safety for herself and her daughter. The emotional and financial challenges she faced as a single mother were immense. Struggling to make ends meet and provide

Debbie with a stable home, Joan began to entertain the idea of taking matters into her own hands.

The combination of her traumatic past and her need to provide for her child led Joan to the criminal world. When she met **Boisie**, an antiques dealer with connections to London's underworld, Joan saw an opportunity. Though morally conflicted, she decided that crime was a way to escape the traps of her past, offering her a chance to finally take control of her life.

The initial steps were small—small-time thefts and schemes to make quick cash—but Joan quickly realized she had a talent for deception and strategy. Her growing reputation as a cunning thief caught the attention of major players in London's criminal world, and Joan's rise to power began in earnest.

Chapter 2: London in the 1980s – A Crime-Fueled City

By the time Joan Hannington began her ascent in the criminal world, London in the 1980s was experiencing profound social and economic change. The city was a hub of both **opportunity and inequality**, creating fertile ground for the rise of organized crime. This era of transformation allowed figures like Joan to capitalize on the growing wealth divide and the culture of excess, particularly within the **criminal underworld**.

The 1980s in Britain, and London in particular, were marked by the policies of **Margaret Thatcher's Conservative government**. Economic reforms—including **privatization**,

deregulation, and an emphasis on individualism—ushered in an era of wealth for some and economic decline for others. **Yuppies** (young urban professionals) came to symbolize the pursuit of financial success, and the mantra of the decade became "**greed is good**".

However, beneath the surface of economic growth, there was a **widening wealth gap**. While the wealthy thrived, many working-class families were left behind, suffering from the decline of traditional industries and growing unemployment. The inner cities saw cuts to public services, rising crime, and deepening social unrest. London's neighborhoods became starkly divided between the glitzy financial districts and struggling working-class communities.

For someone like Joan Hannington—who had grown up in poverty and experienced the sharp end of societal inequality—this landscape of opportunity and deprivation was one she could navigate with sharp intelligence and cunning. London's extremes offered space for those willing to take risks, and Joan, looking to provide for her daughter, seized on the culture of excess.

As London's financial sector boomed, so too did its **criminal underworld**. Organized crime syndicates took advantage of the wealth flowing through the city, targeting everything from banks and jewelry stores to international smuggling operations. The gap between the rich and poor fueled illegal activity, creating a perfect environment for **theft, fraud, and money laundering**.

During this time, crime became increasingly **sophisticated**, with criminal enterprises adopting the very strategies of capitalism that defined the decade. Some syndicates were run like businesses, where money was funneled into **legitimate fronts** such as pubs, nightclubs, and jewelry shops. Joan found herself in the middle of this bustling underworld when she crossed paths with Boisie, a shady antiques dealer who gave her access to some of the most valuable jewels being traded on the black market.

The 1980s also saw the emergence of **high-profile heists**, including **jewel robberies** and bank raids, which were glamorized by the media and fascinated the public. Jewelry stores in London's West End and the **Hatton Garden** district became prime targets for well-planned, daring robberies. For Joan, who had developed a knack for deception and strategy, this presented an opportunity to move from small-time thefts to major heists.

Despite her success, Joan was often underestimated by her male counterparts. Men in the criminal underworld did not expect a woman—let alone a mother—to be capable of pulling off sophisticated heists. However, it was precisely these assumptions that gave Joan her advantage. She often used her gender as a tool of misdirection, allowing her to charm her way into situations and then outsmart her targets.

While the criminal underworld of 1980s London was largely male-dominated, Joan was not the only woman involved in crime during this period, but she was among the few who managed to rise to prominence in such a ruthless environment.

Traditionally, women in the criminal world were seen as either **accomplices** or **accessories**—helping male partners in thefts or fraud schemes without taking center stage. However, Joan broke that mold. Her rise from small-time thefts to becoming a respected figure in London's crime circles was driven by her intelligence, fearlessness, and ability to adapt to dangerous situations.

Joan's success also relied on her ability to leverage her **feminine charm** while operating in a hyper-masculine space. She understood that men in the underworld underestimated women, and she used this to her advantage, often catching her targets off guard. Whether it was swallowing diamonds during a heist or negotiating her share of a job with ruthless criminals, Joan navigated this world with remarkable cunning.

Chapter 3: The Heist Queen Emerges

Joan's first steps into the world of crime were driven by necessity rather than ambition. After leaving her abusive husband, she was faced with the harsh realities of single motherhood and poverty. Desperate to provide for her daughter, Joan took on various low-wage jobs, but they were insufficient to meet her needs. Crime, particularly jewel theft, began to look like a more lucrative option.

Her initial forays into theft were small-scale. Joan started by working at a local **jeweler**, where she quickly recognized the opportunity for profit. She began by stealing small items that she could easily conceal and later pawn for cash. These early thefts were risky, but they provided

Joan with the experience and confidence she needed to expand her operations. She learned the importance of **blending in**, using her unassuming appearance to avoid suspicion. It wasn't long before she realized that she could take on larger, more sophisticated jobs.

Joan soon moved from small-time thefts to larger heists, targeting high-end jewelers in London's West End. However, her most unique tactic—the one that would earn her notoriety—was yet to come.

What truly set Joan apart in the world of jewel theft was her **unorthodox method** of concealing stolen jewels. As her heists became more daring, she realized she needed a way to smuggle stolen goods without getting caught. Her solution was both daring and ingenious: she began **swallowing diamonds** to avoid detection by authorities.

Joan's method involved selecting small but highly valuable diamonds during a heist and swallowing them before making her escape. Once the diamonds had safely passed through her system, she would retrieve and sell them, often for significant sums of money. This tactic not only allowed her to evade capture but also earned her a reputation as one of the most cunning thieves in the city.

This notorious method was risky, but Joan's calm demeanor and attention to detail helped her execute it successfully. She understood the importance of keeping her **nerves under control**, knowing that any sign of anxiety could arouse suspicion. Her ability to manipulate those around her, particularly men who underestimated her, played a key role in her success.

By this time, Joan's name had started to circulate in the underworld, and her heists became more elaborate. But her criminal career was about to take an even sharper turn with the arrival of a man who would become both her romantic partner and her key to even greater wealth—**Boisie**.

Joan's partnership with **Boisie** marked the beginning of her most lucrative period as a jewel thief. Boisie was an antiques dealer with deep connections to the criminal underworld, including contacts with fences who could move stolen goods quickly and discreetly. He saw potential in Joan and admired her intelligence and audacity.

Their relationship was built on **mutual benefit**. Boisie provided Joan with access to a network of high-end buyers, while Joan brought in the goods through her increasingly sophisticated heists. Together, they formed a formidable team, executing jobs that required both careful planning and quick getaways.

Beyond their professional collaboration, Joan and Boisie became romantically involved, though their relationship was far from smooth. Boisie, like many men in Joan's life, was controlling and at times volatile. However, Joan was no longer the vulnerable woman she had once been. She learned to navigate her relationship with Boisie, using it to her advantage while maintaining her independence.

Their relationship was a complicated mix of **love, crime, and power**. On the one hand, Boisie offered Joan the protection and connections she needed to pull off bigger jobs. On the other hand, Joan's growing success gave her the leverage to demand more control over their operations. It was this balance of power that kept their partnership intact, despite the volatility of their personal relationship.

Together, they pulled off some of Joan's most famous heists, including high-profile jewelry thefts from London's most exclusive stores.

Chapter 4: The Glamour and Grit of Crime

Joan's rise through the ranks of London's criminal underworld was swift. By the mid-1980s, she had become a well-known figure in the city's most notorious circles. Her success was built not only on her intelligence and cunning but also on her ability to navigate a world dominated by men. Many underestimated her, assuming that a woman, particularly a mother, would never be capable of such complex and daring criminal activity. Joan took full advantage of these assumptions, using her charm and ability to remain **unnoticed** to pull off some of her most impressive heists.

One of the key factors in Joan's rise was her **partnership with Boisie**, who introduced her to a network of fences and international buyers. Together, they executed increasingly complex heists, often involving meticulous planning and split-second decision-making. Joan's method of swallowing diamonds to smuggle them past security became the stuff of legend, and her reputation as the "Godmother" of jewel thieves solidified.

Despite her growing notoriety, Joan remained fiercely independent. While Boisie provided access to the underworld, Joan ensured that she was never fully reliant on him or any other criminal figure. She was known for her **astuteness in negotiation**, always making sure she got her fair share from every job. This blend of cunning and independence allowed her to maintain control over her operations while navigating the dangerous landscape of London's criminal elite.

At the height of her career, Joan became enamored with the **glamour** that her criminal lifestyle afforded her. Each successful heist brought with it not only wealth but also a sense of power and freedom that she had never experienced before. Joan reveled in the rush of executing the perfect job—the meticulous planning, the tension of the theft itself, and the satisfaction of a clean getaway. For Joan, crime was not just a means of survival—it became an **addiction**.

Her success allowed her to indulge in the finer things in life. Joan began dressing in **designer clothes**, driving luxury cars, and frequenting exclusive venues where wealth and status were flaunted. The stolen jewels she smuggled out of London were often sold for extravagant sums, which Joan used to fund her lifestyle. She enjoyed the spoils of her crimes, but more than the material rewards, Joan was hooked on the **thrill** of the heist. The sense of danger that came with each job heightened the appeal, creating an intoxicating blend of fear and excitement.

Despite this allure, Joan understood that the world she inhabited was perilous. Every job carried the risk of **capture or betrayal**, and as her reputation grew, so did the pressure to maintain her success. The higher she climbed, the greater the stakes became. One misstep could cost her everything—her freedom, her daughter, and her life. Yet, this danger only seemed to fuel her drive. Joan thrived on the adrenaline, always pushing for bigger scores and more elaborate heists.

While Joan's life as a jewel thief was glamorous, her role as a **mother** was never far from her mind. At the heart of her criminal endeavors was a desire to provide for her daughter, Debbie, and give her a better life than the one Joan had endured. However, balancing motherhood with a life of crime proved to be an immense challenge. Joan was often forced to keep her criminal activities hidden from Debbie, creating a double life where she tried to protect her daughter from the dangers of her own choices.

The strain of maintaining this balance was immense. Joan loved her daughter fiercely, but her involvement in the criminal underworld meant that she was frequently away or embroiled in dangerous situations. To shield Debbie from the more violent aspects of her life, Joan sometimes placed her in the care of others, a decision that weighed heavily on her. The tension between her desire to be a present, loving mother and her need to provide through illegal means was a constant battle.

In moments of reflection, Joan often questioned the path she had chosen. She knew that her lifestyle put both her and Debbie at risk, but the pull of the money and the thrill of the heist kept her moving forward. She had been born into poverty, suffered abuse, and struggled to break free from a system that seemed designed to keep her down. In her mind, the heists were a way to reclaim control over her life, to rise above the hand she had been dealt.

Yet, the deeper Joan became involved in crime, the harder it was to protect her daughter from the consequences. By the late 1980s, cracks began to show in her carefully constructed double life. Law enforcement was closing in, and Joan's time as the queen of the underworld was running out. Despite her success, she remained haunted by the fear that her choices would ultimately cost her the thing she valued most—her daughter.

Chapter 5: Power, Fame, and the Cost of Crime

Joan's reputation as the "Godmother" was built on her ability to run **complex operations** with precision, often working alongside men who underestimated her because of her gender. She thrived in this environment, using the assumptions of others to her advantage. By the mid-1980s, Joan had risen to a position of influence, with criminals seeking her out for advice and partnerships in high-stakes thefts.

Her most famous heists involved **jewelry stores in the West End** of London, where she executed daring thefts that netted her hundreds of thousands of pounds in stolen goods. She became a legend not just for her crimes but for the way she **played both sides**—presenting herself as a well-dressed, unassuming woman while simultaneously orchestrating some of the most sophisticated thefts of the decade.

But this rise to prominence came with its own set of challenges. Joan's success put her in the crosshairs of law enforcement, rivals, and even former allies, all of whom saw her growing power as a threat. As she climbed higher in the criminal hierarchy, the constant **fear of betrayal** became a part of her daily life. She knew that in her world, loyalty was fleeting, and the same people who worked with her could easily turn against her if the stakes were high enough.

Joan surrounded herself with the trappings of success: furs, jewels, and fast cars were all part of the image she cultivated. In the media and in criminal circles, Joan became known not just for her crimes but for her extravagant tastes. Her wardrobe was filled with designer clothes, and she was often seen draped in **expensive fur coats**, a symbol of her newfound status.

Joan's **jewel collection** was enviable, consisting of pieces she had either stolen or purchased with her ill-gotten gains. She flaunted her wealth, often hosting lavish parties and spending money freely. To those who knew her only by reputation, Joan appeared to be living a charmed life—one defined by luxury and power. However, the reality was far more complicated. Behind the façade of glamour, Joan was constantly aware that her lifestyle could collapse at any moment.

The fast cars, designer clothes, and expensive jewelry served as both a shield and a trap. They were symbols of her success, but they also drew attention to her activities. Joan was aware that her high-profile lifestyle made her a target, both for law enforcement and those in the underworld who resented her rise. Yet, the allure of her wealth and status was difficult to give up. The line between **self-preservation and indulgence** became increasingly blurred as Joan struggled to maintain her position of power.

By the late 1980s, the **Metropolitan Police** had begun to focus on high-profile jewel thefts, and Joan's name was increasingly linked to these crimes. As her reputation grew, so did the pressure from both **rivals** and **partners** in the underworld. Trust was a rare commodity in Joan's world, and she was acutely aware that anyone could turn on her if it meant avoiding prison or making a quick profit.

Her relationship with **Boisie** exemplified this dangerous dynamic. While they had initially built a strong partnership, based on mutual benefit and shared criminal ventures, cracks began to show as Joan's ambition grew. Boisie, like others, was aware that Joan was becoming too powerful, and this imbalance threatened their relationship. Joan had to navigate not only the risk of betrayal from within her network but also the increasingly aggressive pursuit of law enforcement.

To manage these threats, Joan relied on her **sharp instincts** and **strategic mind**. She knew when to take risks and when to lay low, always staying one step ahead of those who sought to take her down. However, as the years went on, the pressure mounted. The criminal world was built on fragile alliances, and Joan was constantly walking a tightrope between success and disaster. Every successful heist carried the weight of potential betrayal, and each lavish purchase served as a reminder that her freedom was always at risk.

Despite the wealth, power, and influence she had amassed, Joan understood that her position was precarious. She had built an empire based on deception, and while it allowed her to rise to the top, it also meant she was constantly looking over her shoulder. The cost of her criminal life—both in terms of personal relationships and the psychological toll of always being on the run—began to weigh heavily on her. The life of the **Godmother**, while glamorous on the surface, was riddled with anxiety and danger.

Chapter 6: Life Beyond the Heists

The constant pressure of evading law enforcement, managing dangerous criminal alliances, and the internal strain on her personal life began to surface. As with all high-stakes careers, especially one built on crime, the risks eventually caught up with Joan, marking the end of her illustrious run as the "Godmother" of jewel theft. However, life after crime would bring new challenges, from personal losses to brushes with the law, all of which shaped the next chapter of Joan's life.

When Boisie died, it marked a significant turning point in Joan's life. His death left her emotionally devastated, but it also forced her to reflect on her own mortality and the precarious nature of her criminal lifestyle. For years, Joan had thrived on the adrenaline of heists and the thrill of outsmarting the law. Yet, Boisie's death acted as a sobering reminder that the world she inhabited was unpredictable and dangerous.

In the wake of his death, Joan's emotional and mental state began to shift. She no longer found the same satisfaction in her criminal activities. Boisie had been a key part of her life, both personally and professionally, and without him, her operations lacked the same drive. His absence left a void, one that couldn't be filled by more jewels or more wealth. This loss eventually led Joan to reconsider her life's trajectory.

Following Boisie's death, Joan made the decision to **retire from crime**. Her motivations were clear: she had grown weary of the constant pressure and had begun to fear that her luck would soon run out. While Joan had always been adept at evading law enforcement, she knew that continuing down this path would eventually lead to prison or worse. Thus, in the early 1990s, she made the decision to step back from her life of crime and look for new, more legitimate ways to support herself

Joan's **transition from crime** to more legitimate business ventures was not without its difficulties. She moved into **real estate and legal work**, leveraging the connections and wealth she had amassed during her years as a jewel thief. This shift allowed her to apply the same skills she had honed in her criminal career—cunning, negotiation, and a sharp understanding of human behavior—to the world of business. Despite her past, Joan managed to build a new life for herself, albeit one still haunted by the specter of her former life.

While many criminals struggle to transition back into legitimate society after years in the underworld, Joan's intelligence and resourcefulness helped her navigate this difficult shift. She had spent years living a double life, and this ability to adapt allowed her to make a relatively smooth transition into a more lawful existence. However, her past would continue to follow her, as she soon found herself having to deal with the law in a new context.

Even in her retirement, Joan could not entirely escape her criminal past. Her two **brief encounters with the law** after leaving crime behind serve as a reminder of how deeply entrenched she had been in the world of jewel theft. These brushes with the authorities, while not leading to any long-term legal consequences, underscored the precarious nature of her attempts to move beyond her former life.

In one instance, Joan was questioned about her connections to former associates still active in the criminal world. Though she had officially retired, her reputation and past involvement continued to attract attention from law enforcement. Joan had to navigate these situations carefully, ensuring that she did not get drawn back into the world she had worked so hard to leave behind.

Despite these challenges, Joan managed to avoid serious legal repercussions. Her decision to retire from crime, coupled with her ability to maintain a low profile in her later years, allowed her to evade the long arm of the law. However, these encounters served as a reminder that even though she had left the criminal underworld, her past was never truly far behind.

Chapter 7: From Infamy to Pop Culture Icon

In 2002, Joan published her autobiography, *I Am What I Am*, later republished as *Joan*. The memoir was a raw, unflinching account of her life, from her troubled childhood and abusive marriage to her rise as Britain's most notorious jewel thief. Joan's writing provided a window into the **psychological and emotional toll** of her criminal life, while also offering readers a candid look at her motivations and the complexities of living a double life.

Public reaction to Joan's memoir was mixed, but overwhelmingly fascinated. On one hand, many readers were drawn to the **grit and glamour** of her story—her daring heists, luxurious lifestyle, and ability to outwit both the police and her fellow criminals. On the other hand, some were struck by the **humanity** behind the legend. Joan did not shy away from discussing the costs of her choices, particularly the strain they placed on her relationship with her daughter, Debbie.

The memoir allowed Joan to reclaim her narrative. Instead of being remembered only for her crimes, she positioned herself as a **survivor**—a woman who had endured unimaginable hardships and risen above them, even if that meant taking morally ambiguous paths.

The success of Joan's memoir helped pave the way for further interest in her story, culminating in the 2024 ITV series *Joan*. The six-part drama, starring Sophie Turner, took a bold and **stylized**

approach to Joan's life, capturing both the glamour and danger that defined her time as a jewel thief. The series portrayed Joan as a complex character—fiercely independent, cunning, and, at times, ruthless—while also delving into the emotional core of her story as a mother and survivor.

Joan was **actively involved** in the production of the series, ensuring that her story was portrayed with accuracy and depth. She worked closely with the writers and producers to provide insights into her life, particularly the **psychological toll** of her criminal career. Joan's involvement added a layer of authenticity to the series, allowing the filmmakers to portray her not just as a glamorous thief, but as a woman shaped by trauma and survival

One of the key elements that Joan emphasized was the **importance of her daughter, Debbie**, in shaping many of her decisions. The series captured this dynamic, showing how Joan's desire to provide for her daughter often drove her deeper into the criminal world, even as it strained their relationship. This focus on Joan's internal struggles helped balance the portrayal of her as both a **criminal mastermind** and a **mother** trying to protect her family

The production design of *Joan* was also notable for its recreation of the **1980s London underworld**, with its fast cars, designer clothes, and opulent settings. This stylized aesthetic helped create a vivid backdrop for Joan's heists, capturing the mix of glamour and danger that characterized her life.

The casting of **Sophie Turner**, best known for her role as Sansa Stark in *Game of Thrones*, was a significant factor in the series' success. Turner's portrayal of Joan was marked by a **nuanced performance**, capturing both the steely determination and vulnerability that defined Joan's character. Turner embraced the complexity of Joan's life, shifting between moments of charm and cold calculation during her heists, and softer, more introspective scenes as a mother struggling to protect her daughter.

Turner's performance was praised for its ability to bring **empathy and depth** to a character who might otherwise be seen as merely a criminal. She portrayed Joan not just as a thief, but as a woman shaped by her circumstances—someone who had experienced immense hardship but used her intelligence and resilience to rise above it.

Turner's ability to convey Joan's internal conflict, particularly the tension between her criminal ambitions and her love for her daughter, gave the series a powerful emotional core.

The success of *Joan* has reignited interest in Hannington's life, drawing new audiences to her story. Turner's performance, coupled with the show's slick production and focus on the **feminist undertones** of Joan's journey, helped reframe her legacy. Rather than being remembered solely as a criminal, Joan is now seen as a figure who defied societal expectations and fought for survival in a world where she was often underestimated.

Chapter 8: The Godmother's Legacy

In the pantheon of infamous criminals, Joan Hannington stands out not just for her audacious heists but for how she navigated the criminal world with a combination of intelligence, femininity, and survival instincts. Over the years, her story has become a **touchstone in true crime** narratives, particularly those that explore the nuanced lives of female criminals. Joan's ability to defy both societal and criminal expectations has made her a figure of enduring fascination.

Her **memoir** and subsequent involvement in the **ITV series** *Joan* have further solidified her status as a cultural icon. True crime as a genre has often been dominated by stories of male criminals, but Joan's life challenges the traditional narrative, bringing attention to the **gender dynamics** at play in the world of crime. Her ability to outsmart men in both the criminal and legal worlds—men who underestimated her because of her gender—has cemented her place as one of the few female figures who achieved significant power in the criminal underworld.

Moreover, Joan's story has helped **humanize female criminals** in a way that the media has often failed to do. Through her memoir and adaptations of her life, Joan is presented not just as a cold-hearted thief but as a woman shaped by trauma, poverty, and a need to provide for her daughter. Her rise and eventual exit from the world of crime reflects the complexities of survival, particularly for women who find themselves in situations where traditional routes of success and security are unavailable.

Joan Hannington's story has contributed to the evolving portrayal of **female criminals in media**, both in terms of complexity and depth. Historically, female criminals were either cast as **seductresses** or **accessories** to male criminals, rarely given the same agency or backstory as their male counterparts. However, Joan's narrative, especially as portrayed in *Joan*, challenges these stereotypes. She is depicted as a **mastermind** in her own right, operating not through manipulation of men but through her own wit, strategy, and determination.

In the broader context of crime media today, we are seeing more nuanced portrayals of female criminals that move beyond simple tropes. Shows like *Killing Eve* and *Orange is the New Black* have contributed to a more **multi-dimensional portrayal** of women who commit crimes, focusing on their motivations, emotional depth, and the societal pressures they face. Joan's story is very much a part of this trend, offering a narrative that explores the intersection of **gender, crime, and survival** in ways that resonate with modern audiences.

Joan's ability to **balance motherhood with her criminal life** is another aspect that has intrigued audiences. This portrayal pushes against the traditional dichotomy in media where women are either depicted as nurturing mothers or cold-hearted criminals, but not both. Joan's story shows that women, like men, can embody contradictions and complexity. Her love for her daughter Debbie was a driving force behind many of her decisions, even as she navigated the dangerous world of jewel theft.

At the core of Joan Hannington's life is a powerful lesson in **resilience**. From her traumatic childhood to her abusive marriage and her entry into the criminal underworld, Joan constantly faced situations where survival was her only option. Yet, rather than becoming a victim of her circumstances, she used them as fuel to carve out a life of power and influence, albeit in the dangerous world of crime.

Joan's story also highlights the **complicated relationship between power and morality**. In a world where traditional avenues for success were closed to her, Joan found power in crime—a power that gave her autonomy and the ability to provide for her daughter in ways that society had failed to offer. Her life forces us to grapple with the question of whether her criminality was a choice, a necessity, or a mixture of both.

Her legacy reminds us that **crime stories** are not just about the actions themselves but about the people behind them—their motivations, fears, and the worlds they must navigate. Joan's story is one of survival, not just in the literal sense but in terms of **navigating a world designed to keep her down**. Her ability to rise, fall, and rise again speaks to the complexity of human resilience and the many forms it can take, even in the darkest of circumstances.

Chapter 9: Joan Today

Today, Joan resides on the serene **south coast of England**, far from the chaos of London's criminal underworld that once consumed her. Now in her late 60s, Joan has embraced a life of **solitude and reflection**. She no longer courts the media or the spotlight, choosing instead to live out her days in relative anonymity. The scenic, coastal backdrop offers Joan a sense of tranquility that she rarely had during her turbulent younger years. It's a life that stands in sharp contrast to the luxurious but dangerous world she once inhabited.

Joan's quiet life is not only about escaping the past, but also about **rebuilding**. Having left the jewel thievery and criminal enterprise behind, she has transitioned into a life that, while modest, provides her with the security and stability she spent years chasing. While her former life afforded her wealth and notoriety, it also came at the cost of her personal peace and, at times, her family relationships.

For Joan, the south coast represents a form of **self-imposed exile**, a space to reflect on the years she spent evading the law, juggling the dual roles of mother and criminal mastermind, and the toll it took on her psyche and personal life. In interviews, Joan has expressed that while she doesn't miss the constant danger, she occasionally reflects on the thrill of those heists and the life that made her famous.

One of the more delicate aspects of Joan's post-crime life is her relationship with her children. Joan has a **complex relationship** with her daughter, Debbie, who was a central figure in many of her decisions during her criminal career. Joan has often said that her motivation to turn to crime was deeply rooted in her desire to **provide for Debbie** and ensure her daughter would never experience the hardships she endured. However, her criminal lifestyle also put a strain on their relationship, and at times, Joan had to distance herself from Debbie to keep her safe from the dangers of her world.

In recent years, Joan has made efforts to **reconnect with her children**, though this process has not been without its challenges. Debbie, who grew up with the knowledge of her mother's criminal activities, has had a complex relationship with Joan, marked by a mixture of love, resentment, and confusion. Despite these challenges, Joan has expressed that her love for Debbie has always been the core of her life, even when their relationship was at its most strained.

Joan's relationship with her son, **Benny**, has also been an area of focus in her later years. Benny, who has largely stayed out of the public eye, has maintained a closer relationship with his mother. In interviews, Joan has noted that Benny has been more understanding of her choices and has played a supportive role in her life after her retirement from crime.

For Joan, reconnecting with her children has been both a **redemptive and painful journey**. While her past will always cast a long shadow, she remains committed to healing the emotional wounds caused by the years of distance and danger. The process of rebuilding these relationships is ongoing, but Joan has expressed a deep desire to make amends where possible and to create a sense of family that was often lacking during her years as the "Godmother" of crime.

Joan's reflection on her past is filled with **mixed emotions**. On one hand, she is proud of her intelligence, cunning, and ability to survive in a world that was often stacked against her. She has spoken openly about the challenges she faced as a woman in a male-dominated criminal underworld and how she used those challenges to her advantage. Joan does not shy away from acknowledging the **thrill** and **adrenaline** that came with pulling off high-profile heists, nor does she deny that the wealth and luxury she accumulated were powerful motivators.

However, with age has come a more nuanced view of her past. Joan now reflects on the **costs** of her criminal life—the strain it placed on her family, the emotional toll of constantly living in fear of arrest or betrayal, and the eventual loss of people like Boisie, whose death marked a turning point for her. While she enjoyed the spoils of her crimes—luxury cars, furs, and jewels—Joan now admits that these material rewards came at the expense of personal peace and long-term stability.

In various interviews, Joan has expressed a sense of **regret** for some of the choices she made, particularly the way her criminal career impacted her relationship with Debbie. While she does not regret her ability to survive and thrive in a world that offered her few legitimate opportunities, she recognizes that the life of crime came with consequences that extended beyond her own personal freedom.

Ultimately, Joan's reflection on her past is a **balancing act**. She acknowledges both the **empowerment** and **destruction** that came with her life of luxury and crime. While she may no longer be the "Godmother" of jewel thieves, her legacy as a complex figure—one who navigated power, danger, and survival in equal measure—remains.

Chapter 10: The Enduring Fascination with Female Criminals

One of the reasons audiences remain fascinated by female criminals like Joan is because their stories often defy **societal expectations**. Historically, women have been seen as nurturing, passive, or victims of circumstance. However, figures like Joan challenge these stereotypes, demonstrating that women can also be **calculating, ambitious, and powerful**. This subversion of gender norms is at the heart of why female criminals garner so much attention—people are intrigued by women who operate outside the traditional boundaries of femininity.

In Joan's case, her ability to rise through the ranks of London's criminal underworld, outsmarting both her male counterparts and law enforcement, has contributed to her enduring appeal. Her life offers a complex narrative that includes elements of **survival**, **power**, and **agency**, which resonate with audiences who are drawn to stories of individuals who take control of their circumstances, even when that control involves breaking the law.

Moreover, stories of female criminals often blur the line between **victimhood and agency**. Women like Joan are frequently portrayed as both products of their environments—having experienced abuse, poverty, and marginalization—and as individuals who refuse to be victims, using crime as a means of empowerment. This duality creates a rich narrative that captures public imagination. Joan's story, in particular, reflects this tension between being a survivor of her circumstances and a powerful figure who chose to wield control in unconventional and sometimes illegal ways.

Over time, the portrayal of **female criminals in media** has evolved, moving away from one-dimensional depictions of women as either seductresses or passive participants in crime. Instead, media has begun to explore the **complex motivations** behind female criminality, giving these characters greater depth and nuance. This shift is evident in the way Joan's story has been portrayed, particularly in the 2024 ITV series *Joan*, where she is depicted not just as a glamorous thief but as a **mother**, a **survivor**, and a **master strategist**.

Historically, media representations of female criminals often leaned on **gender stereotypes**—women were seen as manipulative or motivated by emotions like jealousy or revenge, often portrayed through the lens of their relationships with men. However, modern portrayals are more likely to explore the **systemic forces** that drive women to crime, such as poverty, lack of opportunity, or abuse. Joan's story, for example, is framed around her efforts to escape her abusive marriage and provide for her daughter, offering a more **empathetic and layered view** of her criminality.

The **true crime genre** has also played a significant role in reshaping how female criminals are viewed. Shows like *Killing Eve* and *Orange is the New Black* have introduced complex female characters who challenge the traditional portrayal of women in crime, making space for nuanced discussions about gender, power, and morality. Joan's inclusion in this evolving narrative speaks to the growing recognition that **female agency** in crime is often more complicated than simple greed or malice. Instead, these stories highlight the **intersectionality** of gender, class, and survival.

The **true crime genre** has exploded in popularity over the past two decades, with audiences devouring books, documentaries, and TV series that explore both historical and contemporary crimes. This growing fascination with true crime, particularly stories that center around complex female criminals, speaks to broader societal shifts in how we view **justice, morality, and identity**.

One reason for the public's obsession with true crime is its ability to provide **catharsis**. These stories allow audiences to confront the darker aspects of human behavior in a way that feels safe—viewers can explore the chaos of criminality without ever being directly involved. Female criminals, in particular, add another layer to this experience. Their stories often involve themes of **rebellion and defiance** against a society that imposes strict limitations on women, which makes them particularly compelling.

Joan Hannington's life as a **female mastermind** in a male-dominated underworld is a prime example of why audiences are drawn to these narratives. Her story reflects both the **fascination with criminal ingenuity** and the **cultural conversation** around women's autonomy and empowerment. At a time when conversations about **gender roles** are evolving, true crime stories like Joan's serve as vehicles for exploring these broader social issues.

Moreover, the **rise of female-focused crime stories** signals a shift in how society perceives women's place in both crime and culture. Rather than being relegated to passive roles, women like Joan Hannington are seen as active agents who shape their destinies—even if that means operating outside the law. This perspective highlights a significant **shift in cultural attitudes** toward female criminals. Rather than being portrayed solely as accomplices or driven by emotional motivations, women like Joan Hannington are now seen as **complex, active agents** capable of shaping their own destinies—even if that means operating outside societal norms and legal boundaries. Joan's story exemplifies how women in crime are no longer passive participants, but individuals who assert **power and autonomy**, often in response to oppressive circumstances.

In a broader sense, this change in how female criminals are portrayed aligns with the evolving discussions around **gender roles** and **empowerment** in contemporary media. Audiences are increasingly drawn to narratives where women break free from the constraints traditionally imposed on them, exploring themes of **agency, survival, and rebellion**. This reflects the wider cultural movements advocating for women's rights and autonomy, creating space for stories that highlight the **complexities of female identity** and the diverse ways women respond to societal pressures.

The rise of **female-focused crime stories** in media and true crime reflects the public's ongoing fascination with the intersection of **gender, power, and morality**. As society continues to grapple with these issues, stories like Joan Hannington's will remain relevant, challenging perceptions and prompting discussions about **the roles women can—and do—play** in shaping their own fates, whether within the bounds of the law or beyond them.

Conclusion: The Price of Power

Joan Hannington's journey began in **desperation and survival**, as she sought to escape an abusive marriage and provide a better life for her daughter, Debbie. But what started as a means of survival quickly escalated into a career of calculated heists, cunning strategies, and high-stakes thefts. Joan rose to prominence in the criminal underworld not simply by luck, but by leveraging her intelligence, charm, and determination. She defied societal expectations of women, using her position as an underdog to outwit both law enforcement and her male counterparts.

Joan's story speaks to the **power dynamics of crime**, especially for women. In a male-dominated underworld, she carved out a niche for herself, proving that she could thrive in an environment where women were typically relegated to secondary roles. Her ability to maintain her independence, negotiate fair terms for her heists, and ultimately control her own destiny made her a formidable figure. Yet, with this power came immense personal cost, not only to Joan herself but also to her family and loved ones.

While Joan's life of crime brought her wealth and power, it also exacted a heavy personal toll. Her relationships with those closest to her, particularly her daughter, Debbie, and her partner Boisie, were strained by the constant danger and secrecy that came with her criminal lifestyle. Joan's desire to provide for her daughter was one of the driving forces behind her criminal endeavors, but ironically, it was also the cause of deep **emotional distance** between them. The life she chose to lead—a life filled with danger and deceit—often kept her away from Debbie, leaving lasting scars on their relationship.

Moreover, Joan's rise to power came with the constant fear of **betrayal and capture**. The threat of arrest and the knowledge that her allies could turn against her at any moment left her in a state of perpetual vigilance. While she thrived on the adrenaline and the rewards of her heists, the psychological strain of always being on the run took its toll. This life of luxury and excitement masked the reality of isolation and fear, as Joan had to protect not only her wealth but her freedom.

The death of Boisie marked a turning point in Joan's life. It was a reminder of the fragility of her world and the personal losses that came with living on the edge. His passing forced Joan to confront the **emptiness** that lay beneath her glamorous facade, leading her to step away from her life of crime. But by then, the damage had been done, both to her personal life and her sense of self.

In her later years, Joan transitioned from a life of crime to a life in the **public eye**. Her memoir, *I Am What I Am*, and the 2024 ITV series *Joan* allowed her to reclaim her narrative, transforming her from a notorious criminal into a **pop culture icon**. Her involvement in the production of the series, as well as the way Sophie Turner brought her story to life on screen, provided Joan with a sense of closure and control over how she was remembered.

The public's fascination with Joan speaks to the enduring allure of **true crime** and the stories of women who defy societal norms. Joan's transformation from jewel thief to media figure is emblematic of how criminals can be both vilified and celebrated, depending on how their stories are framed. For Joan, the transition to a media sensation allowed her to reflect on her life with a degree of detachment, acknowledging both the thrill of her past and the personal costs that came with it

In the end, Joan Hannington's life is a demonstration to the **price of power**. She achieved a level of autonomy and control that few women of her time could, but it came at a significant cost —from a woman who used crime to escape her circumstances to a figure who now stands as a symbol of both empowerment and caution.

Printed in Great Britain
by Amazon